ISBN 978-1-334-82128-8
PIBN 10748446

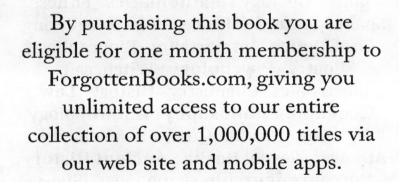

TABLE OF CONTENTS

I. STATEMENT OF THE PROBLEM

President Nixon stated in a message to Congress 17th of
June 1971 that "Narcotics addictions is a problem which affects
both the body and the soul of America...The threat of narcotics
among our people is one which frightens many Americans. It
comes quietly into homes and destroys children, it moves into
neighborhoods and breaks the fiber of community."[1] Heroin is one
the greatest problem producing drug known to mankind.

It has been estimated that in the United States alone
there are over 200,000 heroin addicts. Ten years ago it was
estimated that there were 60,000 heroin addicts in the United
States. In 1969 the number of addicts doubled from the previous
year.[2]

In 1965 there were less than 50,000 arrests in the United
States for heroin related offenses. In 1969 there were 233,690
such arrests. Twenty per cent of these arrests were in suburban
areas where heroin problem had never existed before. During the
last 10 years drug arrest trends for persons under 18 years of

---

[1] Message From President Nixon to the Congress: "President
Calls for Comprehensive Drug Control Program", Department of State
Bulletin, July 1971, p. 65.

[2] Harvey R. Wellman, Drug Abuse: "A Challenge to US - Turkish
Cooperation in the Seventies", Department of State Bulletin,
April, 1971, p. 140.

age has increased 2,500 per cent. In New York City alone
three persons die daily because of heroin related causes.[3]

The growing and spreading abuse of heroin and other
dangerous drugs is causing death and suffering in the United
States and many other countries. The United States is involved
in a world solution to the heroin problem.

Heroin is a product of the gum substance from the opium
poppy flower. This flower is not native to the United States.
As reported to the United Nations in 1968, the world legal
production of opium (exclusive of Communist China) was 993 tons.
Of this India produced 752 tons, the U.S.S.R. 116 tons, and
Turkey 122 tons. According to the best estimates, illicit
production of opium totaled for the claendar year 1968 approximately 1,400 tons. Of this estimate 100 tons were produced
in Turkey.[4] If there is to be a solution to the heroin problem
it will have to be accomplished through international cooperation.
It has been estimated that 70 to 90 per cent of the heroin sold
on the illicit market in the United States originates or is grown
in Turkey.

> "Illicit Turkish opium is of particular importance to
> the United States because much of it ends up as heroin
> in the United States market. Other regions, notably the
> Burma-Thailand-Laos area, with an estimated illicit pro-
> duction of 700 metric tons, are much larger producers;
> but their production is largely consumed locally and until
> now has represented only about 10 per cent of the illicit
> traffic to the United States."[5]

---

[3]Ibid., 141.

[4]Ibid., 144.

Turkey is an important producer of opium, and the United States is an important consumer of illicit Turkish heroin. Turkey has no opium or heroin addiction problems. In Turkey cultivation of the opium poppy has been traditional from time immemorial.

> ..."It is hard for the Turkish Government and people to appreciate the death and suffering which come from use of and addiction to heroin. It is hard for the American Government and people to appreciate the diffi- culties of bringing Turkish opium production under effective control and preventing its diversion to illicit traffickers for processing into heroin and smuggling into the United States."[6]

PROFIT MOTIVE IN HEROIN

10 kilos of Opium Gum on the illegal market in Turkey approximately	$ 438.00
10 kilos of Opium Gum convert into 1 kilo of Morphine approximately	$ 950.00
1 kilo of Morphine is converted into 1 kilo of Heroin in France and sells for approximately	$ 5,000.00
1 kilo of Heroin is sold to the Mafia in the USA for approximately	$ 35,000.00
Mafia will split the Heroin into 1/4 kilos and sell them for approximately	$ 12,000.00
	X 4
	$ 48,000.00
1/4 kilos of Heroin cut and sold in 1 oz. bags for approximately	$ 700.00
16% Heroin makes 45,056 bags, these bags are farther cut until they reach 5% pure heroin and sell on the N.Y. City black market for approximately	$ 281,000.00

---

[6]Ibid., 140.

II. UNITED STATES EFFORTS TO CURTAIL THE
INTERNATIONAL HEROIN PROBLEM

Heroin has no legal or medical use in the United States
and is only sold here to drug abusers. The United States
Government realizes all efforts at home to control the heroin
problem will fail if there is not a world attack on the problem.

History has a long list of international efforts   to
control narcotics. President Theodore Roosevelt in 1909 initiated
a meeting of 13 nations that were involved in international trafficking of narcotics and urged their cooperation in international
efforts to stem the flow of illicit drugs. In 1912 the First
Opium Conference met at the Hague and adopted the International
Opium Convention, making production and distribution of opium
to be limited to medical and science requirements. The League of
Nations took over the responsibility for supervision of the
former agreements that had been made with regard to the traffic
in opium and other dangerous drugs. The Geneva Convention of
1925 established the first international organ with control power
over narcotics.

After World War II the United Nations took over from the
League of Nations the responsibility for overseeing the narcotic

control treaties.   The 1953 Opium Protocol was the first
international attempt directed at controlling the production
of opium.   Seventy-nine nations are now parties to the 1953
Opium Protocol.   It is this treaty that the United States
would like to see made effective.

III. TURKISH PROBLEM IN CURTAILING

THE DRUG FLOW

Turkey and the United States are both signers of the
1953 Opium Protocol.

Under a United Nations convention Turkey is one of the
few nations permitted legally to grow poppies for export. Only
about ten per cent of the world's opium is grown in Turkey. It
has been estimated that eighty per cent of the heroin that enters
the United States originates from the Turkish poppy fields.[7]

The United States had additionally pledged the Turkish
Government $15 million to compensate the Turkish farmers for
loss of production and $20 million to create alternate sources
of income if they will refrain from opium poppy production.
Under strong American persuasion, Turkey decided last year to
ban all growing of poppies on August 31, 1972.[8]

Mr. Harold H. Saunders of the National Security Counsel
Staff stated that the economic assistance to Turkey this year
(1971) has been around $40 million.[9]

---

[7]Nixon, Rodgers, & Meliah, "United States Hail Turkish
Decision to Ban Opium Poppy Production", Department of State
Bulletin, July, 1971, p. 75.

[8]Henry Kamm, "Turkish Farmers See Poverty in Ban on the
Poppy", New York Times, October 3, 1972, p. 1.

[9]Nixon, Rodgers, & Meliah, "United States Hails Turkish
Decision to Ban Opium Poppy Production", Department of State
Bulletin, July, 1971, p. 77.

The annual per capita income in Turkey is $350.00.
The yearly income of a Turkish poppy farmer is not believed
to exceed $500.00. It is believed that a farmer would not
produce in excess of 10 kilograms of opium to sell annually.
At the 1971 price 10 kilograms of opium would bring $128.00
at the legal price and $357.00 when sold to a smuggler's agent.[10]

The delicate leaves of the young poppy plant makes a
delicious salad. The seeds provide oil for the bulk of the
fat in the Turkish diet. The husk of the seeds and other
parts of the plant make feed for the cattle, bread, furniture,
firewood and pharmaceuticals.

As of yet the Turkish poppy farmer states that no one
has told them what they can produce or how they are to employ
their time. The poppy crop has been handed down through many
generations of Turkish farmers. It is the best crop that they
have. The Turkish farmer feels that the United States Government
is putting him in a very bad way.[11]

Since 1967 Turkey has reduced from 21 to 4 the number of
provinces in which it is legal to grow the opium poppy. The
Turkish Government recognizes that as long as opium production
continues in Turkey that it has an obligation to purchase the
entire crop. The Turkish Government has attempted to meet this

---

[10]Henry Kamm, "Turkish Farmers See Poverty in Ban on the
Poppy," New York Times, October 3, 1972, p. 1.

[11]Ibid., 12.

obligation by placing over 1,000 Turkish National police in
the opium growing areas to deter smuggling.[12]

Despite greatly heightened surveillance by the Turkish
Government over the last two years there has not been any reduction in the supply of Turkish opium.

With the two year old reduction in the number of provinces
from 21 to 4 the illicit flow of opium out of Turkey has not
suffered any shortage. The farmers have always sold approximately
one third of their crop on the black market and they state that
1972 has not been an exception. Farmers continue to grow poppies
in many of the regions where Turkish Government has already
outlawed poppy cultivation.

Farmers often plant tall sunflowers facing the road,
behind which the poppies grow as before. Although poppies
growing are easily spotted from the air by plane, low flying
is difficult and planes are scarce.[13]

---

[12]Wellman, "A Challenge to U.S. - Turkish Cooperation,"
p. 145.

[13]Henry Kamm, "Turkish Ban on Poppy: Delayed Impact Seen,"
New York Times, October 10, 1972, p. 1.

IV. TURKISH-UNITED STATES INVOLVEMENT
IN DRUG TRAFFIC

In Turkey the poppy farmer receives about $45.00 for a kilogram of opium gum from the illegal dealer. The opium gum is converted in volume to morphine and heroin at a 10 to 1 ratio. Its price as heroin will increase on the European market to $5,000 per kilo to a wholesale price in New York of $35,000 per kilo to a retail price in New York of $281,000.00 per kilo. In the illegal market the price of 1 kilo of raw opium will have increased 10,000 times between the Turkish farmer and the fix in New York City. The Turkish producer nor the Turkish Economy profit little if any from the illicit marketing of the opium. The huge profits go to the illegal processors.

As of yet the Turkish Government has not been able to establish effective controls of the illegal opium production. Approximately half of the opium produced in Turkey ends up in the illegal markets.[14] The Turkish Government is aware of this problem and that she has not lived up to the commitment she has made under international treaty.

---

[14]Ibid., 14.

The United States recognizes that control of opium
production and the elimination of illegal production and
sale of opium in Turkey is an obligation only that the
Turkish Government can control effectively.

Turkey and the United States are involved together in
this international problem. Turkey is the producer and the
United States is the consumer. Both harbor illicit traffickers.
Both are parties to international treaties on narcotic control.
They are also friends and allies, bound by solemn obligations
of mutual assistance in defense and development.

With approval of the Turkish Government the United States
has stationed professional narcotic agents in Turkey. They
work closely with the Turkish control authorities to facilitate
the exchange of information, experiences, and techniques.

Turkey and the United States have both worked together
in and through the United Nations Commission on Narcotic Drugs.
Jointly they have urged and supported resolutions to control
the production, manufacture, and exports of narcotic drugs.

V. OTHER NATIONS EFFORTS TO CONTROL
THE DRUG PROBLEM

On September 28, 1971 Thailand signed a memorandum
pledging their efforts to control and eliminate the flow of
narcotics from and through Thailand with the United States.[15]

On September 23, 1971, the government of Laos made it
unlawful to engage in the manufacture, trading, and trans-
portation of opium and its derivatives including heroin.[16]

On August 6, 1971, French President Pompidou proposed
to the other five members of the European Economic Community
and the United Kingdom that they consider ways to combat
narcotics trafficking.[17]

November 22nd to 25th, 1971 the Australian Government
sponsored a conference of Southeast Asian countries for the
purpose of improving narcotics controls on regional bases.[18]

President Thieu of the Republic of Viet Nam has encouraged
tough antinarcotics laws to the South Viet Nam legislature.[19]

On August 11, 1971, the Deputy Attorney General of Mexico
reported that 10,356 fields of opium poppy has been destroyed,

---

[15]Nelson Gross, "International Narcotics Control Summary
1971", Department of State Bulletin, February 1972, p. 165.

[16]Ibid., 166.

[17]Ibid.

[18]Ibid.

[19]Ibid.

176 pounds of crude opium, 116 pounds of heroin and 319 pounds of cocaine has been seized.[20]

We must have international cooperation to effectively curb the heroin problem. The United States considers the heroin addiction problem of American citizens an international problem of grave concern.

President Nixon has proposed as an international goal, an end to opium production. Because opium is needed for medical purposes and it is a legitimate source of income in some countries the United States is pressing ahead with three programs. First, develop synthetic substitutes for opium derivatives. Second, assist countries in their effort to end illicit drug processing and trafficking and illegal opium production. Third, make national and international controls more effective.[21]

Because funds have not been immediately available in the United Nations the United States has given funds and earmarked them for immediate measures against drug abuse. The problem of drug abuse is the United States today but could be that of any country tomorrow.

Drug abuse is a continuing challenge to international relations.

---

[20]Ibid.

[21]Harry R. Wellman, "Department Discusses International"

JACK E. SUTHERLAND
Chaplain (Maj) USA
5-16-C-22-73-1
14 May 1973

BIBLIOGRAPHY

Gross, Nelson. "International Narcotics Control Summary 1971."
Department of State Bulletin. February, 1972. Pp. 163-174.

Gross, Nelson. "Recent Activities in International Drug Control."
Department of State Bulletin. November, 1971. Pp.600-604.

Hough Jr., George P., Alvin E. Stack, & Alexander Limont. "International Drug Abuse Manual." A Guide for Regulatory Officials.
Philadelphia. Pa., Smith Kline & French Laboratories, Copy-
righted 1969.

Ingersoll, John E. "U.S. Proposes New U.N. Action Program Against
Illicit Narcotics." Department of State Bulletin. October
1970, Pp. 492-497.

Ingersoll, John E. "U.S. Urges Stronger Multilateral Commitments
to Narcotics Control." Department of State Bulletin.
November 1971. Pp. 600-604.

Kamm, Henry. "Turkish Ban on Poppy: Delayed Impact Seen." New
York Times. October 10, 1972. Pp. 1 & 14.

Kamm, Henry. "Turkish Farmers See Poverty in Ban on the Poppy."
New York Times. October 3, 1972. Pp. 1 & 12.

Message From President Nixon to the Congress: "President Calls
for Comprehensive Drug Control Program," Department of
State Bulletin. July 1971. Pp. 58-65.

Nixon, Rodgers, & Meliah. "United States Hails Turkish Decision
to Ban Opium Poppy Production." Department of State
Bulletin. July 1971. Pp. 74-77.

Rodgers & Khoman. "U.S. and Thailand Sign Memorandum of
Understanding on International Narcotics Control."
Department of State Bulletin. October 1971. Pp. 411-413.

Rodgers, William P. "Secretary of State Discusses New Cabinet
Committee on International Narcotics Control." Department
of State Bulletin. October 1971. Pp. 357-361.

United Nations. Office of Public Information, Radio and Visual
Services. "Perspective Seventy-two", Drug Abuse "No. 21,
May 24, 1972. Pp. 1 - 8.

13

14

United Nations. Press Section, Office of Public Information
Conference in Geneva Adopts Protocol Amending 1961
Convention on Narcotic Drugs (SOC/NAR/133), March 29,1972.
Pp. 1 - 15.

United Nations. Public Inquires Unit. International Organs
Dealing with the Control of Narcotic Drugs. June 1972. P. 1.

United Nations. Public Inquires Unit. Interpol Versus the
Underworld of Narcotics. May 1970. Pp. 1 - 6.

United Nations. Public Inquires Unit. Office of Public
Information. The International Control of Narcotics.
May 1970. Pp. 1 - 4.

United Nations. Public Inquires Unit. Office of Public
Information. LSD New Menace to Youth. May 1972.
Pp. 1 - 4.

Wellman, Harry R. "Department Discusses International Aspects
of President Nixon's Drug Control Program," Department
of State Bulletin. August 1971, Pp. 157-160.

Wellman, Harvey R. Drug Abuse: "A Challenge to U.S. - Turkish
Cooperation in the Seventies," Department of State
Bulletin. April 1971, Pp. 140-146.

CPSIA information can be obtained
at www.ICGtesting.com
Printed in the USA
BVHW071018141218
535632BV00019B/900/P

9 781334 821288